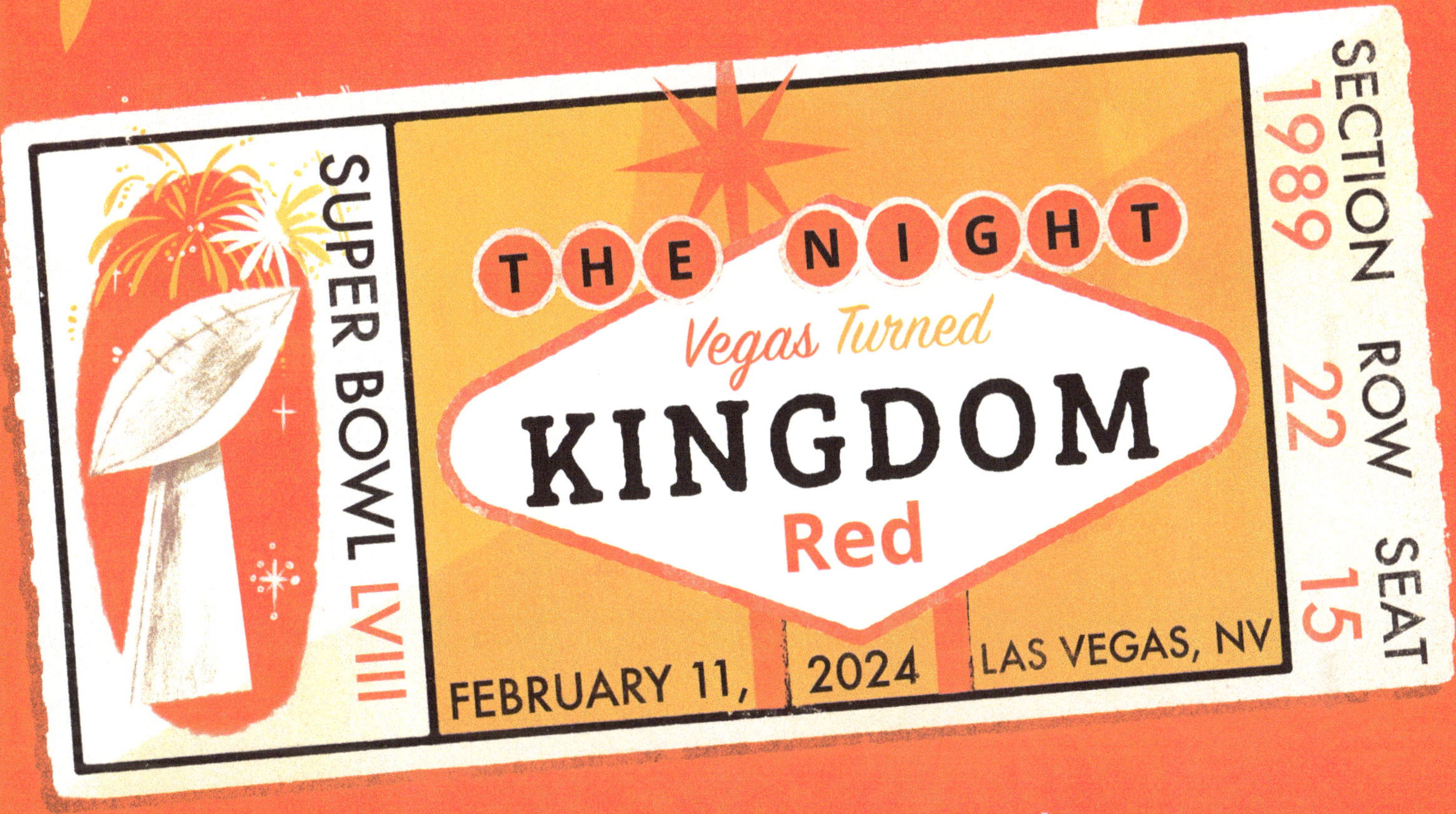

THE NIGHT Vegas Turned KINGDOM Red

SUPER BOWL LVIII • FEBRUARY 11, 2024 • LAS VEGAS, NV
SECTION 1989 • ROW 22 • SEAT 15

Written by Jason Sivewright

Illustrations by Kevin & Kristen Howdeshell

With Fireworks over Tampa, and some in LA.
The world thought the Chiefs just might go away.
But there was little the rest of the world could do,
Except to be left feeling 2022.

'Twas the last year in five, at Super Bowl time,
The Chiefs weren't a team with their dreams still alive.
And with the GOAT at QB and the GOAT at tight end,
The Chiefs had been trouble from the day they walked in.

But the year hadn't gone as Chiefs fans had planned.
With passes bouncing out of Chief's player's hands
And a big lump of coal on a cold Christmas Day,
Was a home game that wrapped up the Raiders' way.

All KC fans sounded a similar tone,
Wishing the REAL Chiefs would come to the phone.
By the day after Christmas, something new had begun
And the Kingdom got set for a wild playoff run.

First, Miami's McDaniels brought the Cheetah to town.
But the water was frozen, so the Dolphins went down.
Then, the Chiefs had to deal with the Buffalo mob,
But Mahomes proved to be just the man for the job.

The Ravens were next. Though Lamar made some plays,
KC left them behind in a **lavender haze.**
'Twas the Super Bowl again for Coach Reid and his men,
Cause they kept winning games no one thought they could win.

First, Miami's McDaniels brought the Cheetah to town.
But the water was frozen, so the Dolphins went down.
Then, the Chiefs had to deal with the Buffalo mob,
But Mahomes proved to be just the man for the job.

The Ravens were next. Though Lamar made some plays,
KC left them behind in a **lavender haze.**
'Twas the Super Bowl again for Coach Reid and his men,
Cause they kept winning games no one thought they could win.

Then, one Vegas night, the Niners lined up to fight,
Hoping the Kingdom would crumble overnight.
This game would declare a dynasty dead,
Or it would be the night Vegas turned Kingdom red.

55 YARDS!

First, San Fran's McCaffrey took to the ground.
The football, he hoped, would be kept safe and sound.
But he fumbled, and the Chiefs pulled it out of the pile.
Mahomes took the field with his own showtime style.

But the offense just couldn't get out of the woods.
So the Niners kicked a field goal, it was up and was good.
The kick was the longest in a Super Bowl game.
But that record was one that was soon to be changed.

Down three, Pop Pacheco rumbled and raced,

To place a score on the board where there was a **blank** space.

But you must hold the football both high and then tight,

Or the Niners can make it a very long night.

So Pacheco fumbled, too, with the ball at the nine,
Leaving Chiefs **chasing shadows in a grocery line.**
While Purdy and San Fran had tricks up their sleeves,
A wide receiver pass for a 10–0 lead.

The first half was **cruel** to Mahomes and his men.
The Chiefs needed to score and begin once again.
With the clock winding down, they marched down the field.
A field goal from Butker meant the Chiefs would not yield.

The second half, for the Chiefs, began with a thud.
A Niners interception made their first drive a dud.
With the Chiefs down by seven, the ball bounced between teams.
Chiefs fans wondered why Bosa's boys were so mean.

But Coach Reid kept scheming, though Travis did pout.
Butker blasted a field goal from 57 yards out.
That record-setting kick was the Chiefs' way to say
That the king wasn't dead, 'cause KC came to play!

Kansas City's Townsend toed a towering punt;
Then, the whole Niners nation gave out a great grunt.

The ball bounced from a foot to the Chiefs like a gift.

Mahomes passed to Marquez for a score that was swift.

But San Fran struck back with a quite Purdy pass.

Their touchdown celebration wasn't one that would last.

For the kick that came after was blocked by Chenal.
And what would come next, both teams knew all too well.

Another field goal from Butker tied the game at sixteen.
Which team would be left with swept-away dreams?
While the other would party like it's **1989**
Each team scored three more, so it was OVERTIME!

Overtime coin flips
depend on the call.

Not just heads or tails,
but who gets the ball.

Take the ball first;
you could burst to the lead,

But your opponent can answer
and answer with speed.

KC lost the toss, and they started to leave.
Then the Niners said something they couldn't believe.

"They want the ball," said Mahomes
in a jubilant way.

"They can have it,"
was all the Big Yeti could say.

WHA?!

OK!

San Fran took the ball and drove down to the nine.
Then Stone Cold Jones showed up big, just in time.
A short field goal kick put the Niners up three.
With all cards on the table, now the Kingdom could see...

A clear path to victory.
A touchdown to win.

That's when the Mahomes
effect began to set in.

The Chiefs drove the field
with rhythm and rhyme

Pacheco reached for first down
but fell short of the line.

Fourth and one's might be harder for somebody else,
But Mahomes just decided to do it himself.
As he ran for first down, all the chips started falling.
It was like all KC heard a dynasty calling.

Not a single dropped ball, pass to Kelce, then Rice.

Then Marquez. Then Pacheco. It all worked just as nice.

As the clock dwindled down, with the Niners fans' souls,
Big Yeti pushed forward for a Chiefs FIRST AND GOAL!

If you would have said on that cold Christmas Day,
The Lombardi would soon be just one play away,
Few would have believed you, at least not for a while.
But I guess that the Chiefs just don't go out of style.

"Tom and Jerry" was the last play in Mahomes' ears.
Of a season, some said, just wasn't their year.
Hardman jetted out right, and the pass found him true.
I guess you can struggle then win it all, too.

The parade filled the streets with joy and then tears.
A true celebration of a year of all years.
Which proved of the Chiefs and The City, in fact,
No matter what happens we will ALWAYS bounce back.

The parade filled the streets with joy and then tears.
A true celebration of a year of all years.
Which proved of the Chiefs and The City, in fact,
No matter what happens we will ALWAYS bounce back.

www.ingramcontent.com/pod-product-compliance
Lightning Source LLC
Chambersburg PA
CBHW061942130526
44582CB00042B/95